Vintage

 Crafts

75 Do-It-Yourself Decorating Projects Using Candles, Colors, and Other Flea Market Finds

Author & Photographer: Clara Lidström

Translated by Anette Cantagallo

Skyhorse Publishing

Contents

To Make Something Out of Nothing

"How do you have time to craft so much?" is a question I am asked regularly, often with an almost reproachful tone. To me, the question is the wrong one. Rather, people should wonder how I can handle not tinkering and crafting even more than I already do. I relax with creativity and crafts. After an intense period of work, I wind down by setting up the sewing machine and putting together a skirt, or by taking out the paint cans and updating a picture frame. When my brain is so overworked that it overheats, handicraft comes like a refreshing bath. I'm hardly alone in this experience.

But why do I spend so much time making things that I can buy in the store? Yeah, why? Why do some people tinker with cars when there are auto mechanics handy? Why do some people cook their own dinner when there are ready-made meals available in the grocery store? Why do some people insist on playing soccer when they can watch professional games directly on the television?

Maybe because people have always had a longing to do things themselves—to test their wings. At a time when most work assignments are abstract, when the results are often only visible on a computer screen, when there's a wide gap between those who make the decisions and those who are told to perform them, it can be a relief to do something that gives immediate, tangible results. I don't think it's any more complicated than that. Before, crafting was done out of necessity—now out of desire. And this is the beauty of it. Creating and crafting should be fun! My Grandmother Bede once said that the best thing to do was to create something out of nothing. I share that mindset.

So what should I make when my fingers itch? How do I bargain at the flea market and how the heck should I make my home cozier? During my years as a blogger, I've received many questions from readers seeking practical help, inspiration, and tips on how they can make their homes a little more personal and unique. I've collected my best answers in this book.

I prefer projects that I can do without bankrupting myself at the craft store. When I improve my home, I use things that I bought at a flea market or something that's been lying around at home—knickknacks like little tin pots. They might not even be that nice looking. Magic is made when you make something unique out of nothing special. My wish is that my readers will be inspired to do the same. Look around your house—use your imagination! Let your creativity run free and discover that crafting is actually purely therapeutic.

Clara

Commandments of Crafting

I hear many people say that they'd love to create something with their hands, but they don't know what to make. People seem to sit on a lot of pent-up creativity that never gets a chance to come out. I think this is a shame, and so I've gathered my best advice to anyone wanting to get crafting.

- **Hoard materials.** It's hard to be creative when you have nothing to work with, so it's a good idea to have materials ready and on hand when inspiration comes. Actually, it's required for inspiration to come at all. Personally, I hoard fabric pieces, picture frames, boxes, and ribbons from the flea market, even though initially I may not know what to use them for.

- **Collect scraps.** Cans, gift wrap, ribbons, old shawls, newspaper clippings, and broken brooches . . . Old becomes new once you fix it up a bit.

- **Begin with something existing.** It's much easier to start with something you already have instead of creating something completely new from scratch. Alter an existing skirt instead of making an entirely new one. Or why not make a miniskirt from a pillowcase? This way you'll learn to create step by step, and nothing will become excessively difficult.

- **Shorten the distance to the start.** Keep your crafting supplies nearby as often as possible. When I see a pile of thread spools, my imagination starts racing. And if the sewing machine is set up already, it's much easier to get started.

- **Don't be too obsessed with how you "ought" to do it.** I have no idea how I "should" sew a pillow case or repaint a chair. I try and see—it can't get worse than going wrong! If I follow instructions too strictly, I get so anxious that I don't dare do anything and the creative process becomes a chore rather than a joy.

- **Avoid craft stores.** Or rather, go to be inspired—but don't buy everything there. Craft stores are often too darn expensive. A dozen fabric flowers for scrapbooking can cost you fifteen bucks, but at the flea market you can find more unique options for less than a dollar.

- **New perspectives give new ideas.** Try turning a lampshade upside down and see what happens. Drape a fun fabric on a chair you haven't thought about dressing. Stack objects on top of one other and see if you can't find new uses for them. Put things in new places. Stand on your head and take a look at your home.

- **Accept that nothing will be as you imagined.** The final result is not worse—just different.

- **And remember**—creativity is a muscle that strengthens when you exercise it. Don't wait for a flash of genius; that will come when you're in the midst of creation.

Good to Have at Home

To create and be creative you need some tools
and materials, so I put together a list of things
that I think are good to have in the home. There
are a lot of things—but you don't need to buy
everything at once. Just like your wardrobe, you
can build your inventory gradually. All of these
items tend to be available for cheap at the local
home improvement store. Or you could just bor-
row from a friend's toolbox.

For Paper Crafts
Paper scissors, paper, glue, tape, wallpaper glue,
applicators, brushes of different thicknesses,
wallpaper remnants, scrapbook paper, book-
marks, and clippings from old newspapers.

For Textile Crafts
Pins, sewing needles, fabric scissors, thread in
the most common colors, measuring tape, fabric
glue, staple gun (a powerful model capable
of stapling into wood—to upholster a piece of
furniture or headboard, for example), fabric
remnants, fun ribbons, elastics, and buttons
(remove these from old garments before you
discard them).

Other Things that Are Good to Have
Wire cutters, flat pliers, hammers, nails in two
sizes, Phillips head screwdriver, slotted screwdriver, screws in two sizes, ruler, wire in two
thicknesses (for jewelry and wreath making, for
example).

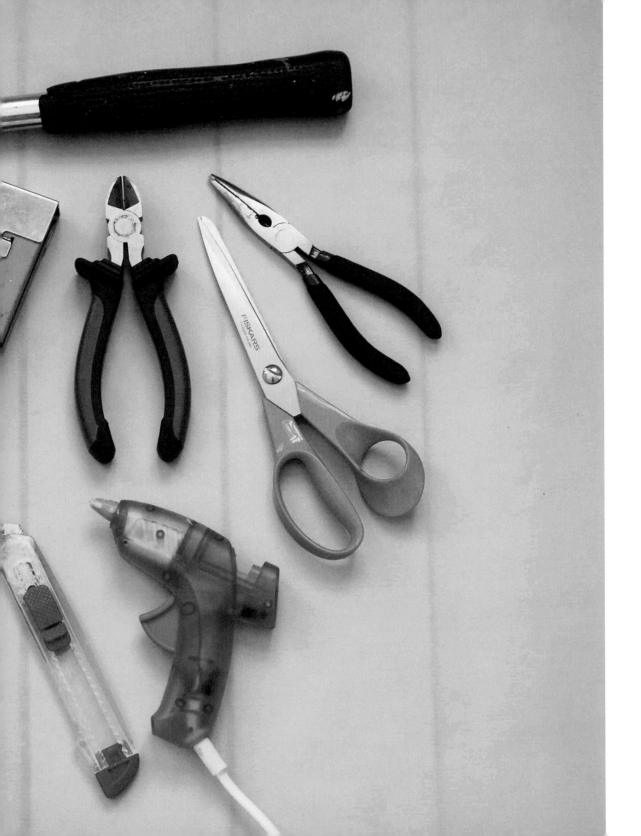

Bedroom

The bedroom should be a quiet and peaceful place, a haven for beauty sleep. Yet, too often it's strewn with dirty laundry, strange-looking ear-plugs, and books scattered in messy piles. This is when you'll need to have a good amount of storage space to tuck away the mess; that way you won't have to look at it.

I love cozy fabrics and love to have pretty rugs to put under my feet. I'll make the bed with lots of blankets and pillows; a bed can never have too many pillows! Number one goes under the head, number two on top, number three goes to the bedmate, and number four gets lost by the feet. Number five is to throw when the dog wakes up in the morning and barks. (I always miss, though.) Hence pillow number two—reliable protection against noise.

Instead of a blanket, you can have a flea market bargain-quilt. In years past, companies made fun quilts—floral, polka dot, and plaid in absolutely hysterical color combinations. Today, they're always white. Stylish perhaps, but certainly boring. I've often heard people say that it's disgusting to re-use other people's linens. So it amuses me to no end to think that these same people, with good appetite, eat vegetables that are grown in cow shit.

The Bed

Our bed is a lovely thing. Mostly I love the gorgeous headboard. When we moved in, there were some old mirror doors left behind in our attic, and I used these to build a headboard. Three mirror doors create a really magnificent headboard, but two fit well with a standard 70-inch wide bed. I simply leaned them against the wall and slid the bed against them. The bed works as a stopper and prevents the doors from tipping over. If you only have one door, you can lay it down long-ways and use it as a slightly lower headboard. Consoles on the bottom and two screws hold the end cap to the wall.

Champagne in Bed

As a side table, I use an auction find: an old Champagne box from Moët & Chandon. I bought wheels from the auto shop and fixed them on with screws, so the side table's easy to move. On top I've stacked two old chests that I inherited from a relative. I like that the paint is abraded and a little drab. And I love that the side table is so tall! I put my alarm clock at the very top so I can't turn it off in my sleep.

Decorative Sugar Boxes

The side table in our guest bedroom consists of a sugar box standing on its side, filled with books. Side tables in particular are often cluttered with books anyway, so why not give them the lead role? This side table can fit a large number of books.

Bed Cover of Kitchen Towels

Old towels are simultaneously pieces of art and artifacts of women's history. Here, I have made a patchwork of my grandmother's old towels. It's a bit fiddly and requires a bit of care to make. It's also important that the lining is washed and shrunken. It's better to use polyester thread as it doesn't shrink the same way that cotton thread does, and sew with a stitch length of one-tenth of an inch.

Instructions: Place the towels on the floor to get an idea of the best composition. Since the towels are of different sizes, I chose to sew them so that they overlapped; in this way, the outer edges of the quilt form straight lines. Pin a few of the towels at a time and sew them together with a straight stitch (it's easier if you start from a corner). Place three layers of padding on the floor. Place the lining on top of it with the right side facing the right side of the quilt top. Pin the three layers of padding to the lining and quilt top and sew around all the edges, keeping a ⅜-inch seam allowance. Leave an opening of about 16 inches, so that you can turn the blanket the right way out. Press the seam allowance with an iron. Then, turn the cover right side out so the padding is now inside the quilt. Hand-sew the opening closed. In order to keep the padding from lumping in the laundry, you may want to sew through all three layers in some places. Follow the seams in the towels and sew together the quilt, padding, and lining fabric.

WHAT YOU NEED:

- 16 towels (for a twin bed)
- padding
- lining
- sewing machine
- tape
- polyester thread
- needles and pins
- iron

Waffles in Bed

A waffle breakfast is really luxurious. This recipe for crisp waffles comes from my Grandma. I love to eat them with whipped cream and a dollop of sour blackcurrant jam.

For about 10 Waffles:
1 ⅔ cups (400 ml) flour
1 ⅓ cups (300 ml) water
1 ⅔ cups (400 ml) heavy whipping cream
a pinch of salt
butter
whipped cream and jam for serving

Instructions: Whisk flour, water, and salt to a smooth batter. Allow the mixture to swell at room temperature for one to two hours. Whip the cream until really fluffy and pour it into the batter. Brush the waffle iron with a little butter and cook the waffles.

TIP:
Candle wax stains on textiles are a real nightmare. The best way to get rid of them is to break away the wax, and then cover the stain with paper towels. Iron over the paper on low heat. Keep replacing the waxy paper towels with clean ones, until the wax is sucked up. Then apply stain remover and wash as usual.

Nice Lighting

Good lighting is a story in itself. A whole school, actually. Myself, I can turn the lights on and off forever before finding the right balance, even when I am invited over to a friend's house. Those awful energy-saving lamps will not enter my house—the cold flickering light gives me a headache. I would rather the place be completely dark! There is nothing like the shine from a good old light bulb! I save the increase in electricity consumption by shutting the lights off regularly.

For an ordinary bedroom, I think between five and seven different light sources are suitable. Remember to place lamps at different levels so they're not all at the same height. A ceiling lamp can used for cleaning, a reading lamp by the bed, cozy-lamps in the window, and perhaps a few small lights that illuminate a bookshelf or a table. If they can be dimmed, it's even easier to get the lighting exactly the way you want. Additionally, I love candles and display them everywhere in the house.

Lamps are quite expensive to buy new, but they make a perfect secondhand purchase. You may need to update the plug to the modern style. If you're worried about doing this yourself, ask for help! An electrician won't charge a lot for this. Otherwise, it's easy to learn to do it yourself. If you're careful, there are usually no problems. Modern plugs are can be found at your home improvement store.

Vintage LED Light Strings

The light string above the bed is vintage-pimped with cute cups. It provides perfect, cozy lighting without risk of overheating or becoming a fire hazard.

Instructions: Stand the paper cups upside down and, using a utility knife, make an X in the bottom center. Make sure the hole is not too large; the bulb should just about fit through. Put the cardboard cups on the light string. Hang it up and light it!

Blazing Yellow Pinewood Lamp

Old pinewood lamps are common at flea markets. They may feel a bit gloomy, but with a little bit of color, they can become really pretty. With a few layers of yellow paint, this handmade pinewood lamp was revitalized.

Before you start painting, it's a good idea to cover the lower part of the cord with masking tape, and wipe the lampshade clean with a damp cloth and some detergent. Then all you have to do is paint the lamp and set it out to dry. Several layers of paint may be necessary because untreated wood absorbs a lot of pigment.

The Prettiest Storage

I love the idea of a linen cabinet neatly filled with folded linens and scented by fragrance sachets. Maybe that's because my own linen cabinet rarely looks that way? When I was a child, I hated my bedroom's wall-mounted wardrobe made with plastic covered plywood; it was so far from the tidy, romantic linen cabinets that decorated my grandma's guest room. In my house, I've banned these modern-day abominations, and instead, I put together some old linen cabinets and wardrobes to make an effective storage system (see photo on page 31). If you place them close together, they'll form a cohesive unit. On top of my wardrobe, I've stacked hatboxes, trunks, and wallpapered shoeboxes. These are ideal for storing things that I don't use very often.

Scrapbooked Linen Cabinet

This old linen closet was originally a drab brown. I painted it with plain, white wall paint, and then I used scrapbook paper to wallpaper the glass on the door. Standard wallpaper works wonderfully too.

Never throw away wallpaper remnants. With leftovers, you can decorate a dollhouse, wrap beautiful packages, make unique invitations, or transform boring boxes into decorative storage.

Instructions: Clean the surface that is to be papered. You can use a damp cloth and a little bit of dish detergent. Wipe dry with a towel.

Measure the area you want to decorate and draw the dimensions on a regular sheet of white paper. Cut the white paper along the trace marks. Put the white paper on the back of the wallpaper and, using the cut-out as a stencil, trace the edges with a pencil.

Cut out the wallpaper, and apply wallpaper paste generously to the cabinet and the back of the wallpaper. Press the wallpaper on the cabinet from the top to the bottom, and remove the bubbles that appear. Allow to dry. After several hours when the wallpaper has dried, you can cover it with a layer of clear lacquer so it attaches better. This will also make it dirt-resistant.

TIP!

- You can get wallpaper remnants if you ask nicely at a paint shop. Sometimes they have old wallpaper sample books that are about to be discarded. These are perfect for folding into bags, making beautiful cards, or as shown here, pimping furniture. There are also stores online that sell wallpaper samples by the yard.

- Make your own wallpaper paste: Boil 1 ⅔ cups (400 ml) of water in a saucepan and add slightly less than half a cup (100 ml) of sugar. Let simmer until the sugar has dissolved. Remove the pan from the heat and let it cool. Mix 1 ⅔ cups (400 ml) of water with 3 tablespoons of potato flour. Pour the flour mixture into the sugar-water, and let it simmer on the stove.

- A wallpaper brush facilitates the wallpapering and helps to remove air bubbles.

WHAT YOU NEED:

- a dash of detergent
- white paper (use a roll of tracing paper if there is a larger surface area to be wallpapered)
- wallpaper or scrapbook paper
- wallpaper paste
- translucent lacquer

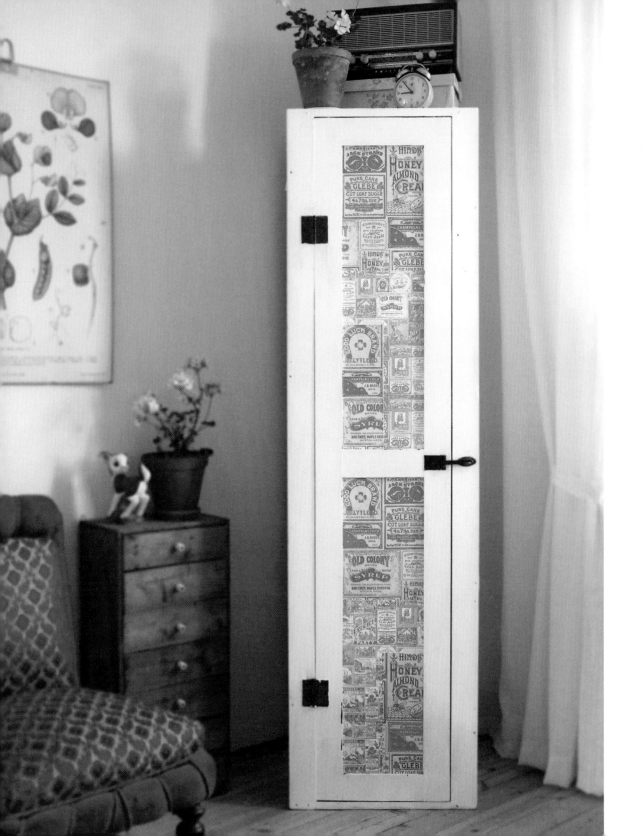

Revitalize a Worn-Out Cabinet

Give a worn-out cabinet new life by using masking tape and paint.

Instructions: Wipe furniture clean with a damp washcloth and a little detergent. Wipe dry. Use masking tape to make a pattern; it's just like painting a wall. I made this pattern by taping the surfaces that I didn't want paint on, and I left the rest of the surface exposed. Be sure to press your finger down along the edges of the tape to prevent ink from seeping under it. Paint one layer with the brush. Let dry and paint a second layer. Teak really absorbs the pigment, so expect to paint 3–4 layers. Carefully remove the masking tape before the last coat of paint has dried.

Potpourri

Make your linen closet extra luxurious, and keep moths and pests away with sachets filled with lavender. Your closets will smell like summer all through the winter. If you don't want to sew, you can use beautiful old handkerchiefs instead.

Instructions: Cut out a square of thin cotton fabric. Zigzag stitch along the edges. Add a little dried lavender (I use home-grown from the flowerbed) in the center of the fabric. Fold the fabric and tie it with a pretty ribbon so that it becomes a small bag.

Silhouette Frames

I found these adorable mini-frames at a flea market for a dollar each. Small silhouettes seemed the perfect motif. I sketched profiles in pencil and filled them in with black ink—simple as that! If you're unsure of your hand, you can instead print silhouette pictures from the Internet. Just Google it.

My Well-Stocked Closet

When I was eleven, I saw *Grease* and fell headlong in love with the '50s silhouette: wide skirts, slim waist, and a whole lot of spin. The first time I saw such a dress was at a secondhand store. Pink silk, tulle skirt, and a beautifully decorated bodice. But it cost $55—way too much to pay for a dress that I would never use, my mother said. And I didn't protest, because I knew my mother was right—I never would have used it. I was too much of a coward! Today, I'm no coward when it comes to clothes, and I basically only wear dresses. I don't even own a pair of pants. They sit so uncomfortably tight that I can't eat or breathe. In a fifties-era dress, however, the tummy gets to bulge as much it needs to, so long as it's below the waistband.

Although that was thirteen years ago, I still sometimes fret over that tulle dream and all the other goodies I've missed out on over the years when I wasn't quite so eagle-eyed for bargains nor as quick-thinking in my creativity.

This is usually the problem when shopping at flea markets. You really have to hunt energetically for bargains—otherwise you'll miss out. I'm slowly learning that I only regret the things I don't buy—never the purchases I actually make. Worst case scenario, if I don't like something I buy, I'll usually just donate it.

TIP!

- To store vintage dresses, hang them up. They hold their shape better this way.
- Wash them by hand to protect the delicate fabric.
- Be sure to wash away any traces of deodorant after wearing, since it can discolor the fabric.
- Secure the buttons carefully. Replacing a lost button on a vintage garment is almost impossible.

Storage Basket for Shoes

Don't hide your favorite shoes! With a storage basket, you can put them on display and keep them aired out and away from shoe-loving dog teeth.

My Beloved Dresses

THE HOUSE DRESS

A yellow dress with white polka dots in a house dress style needs a few accessories to keep it from feeling out of date. I always pair mine with a sharp pair of heels! This dress cost me $10 at a secondhand store—an amazing bargain!

'50S NOSTALGIA

My sister helped a friend clear out her attic. Among heaps of scraps and dust, she found several pretty '50s-era dresses for me. My favorite is this green one with a big bow at the neck.

THE SUMMER DRESS

I bought the ultimate summer dress at a boot sale. A '50s design in '80s fabric with an incredible spin in the skirt. I have to be careful on windy days! The price tag was $6.

'80S

I found this '80s dress with a pen skirt in fragile fabric at a store called Beyond Retro. It's a timeless, classic cut in an absolutely hysterical pattern. I only paid $30, but I feel like a million bucks in it!

THE PARTY GOWN

When I graduated, I searched every corner of Stockholm for a fun vintage dress. In my last store of the day, in a dodgy nook of the city, I found this silk gem for $120. I don't think there's a dress I've had more fun in! I wear it to all of my fanciest celebrations and parties.

A MARITIME FIND

I stopped at a summer flea market and this sailor dress caught my eye immediately. The woman who was selling it had worn it in her youth and she chuckled heartily about the wild times she'd had in it.

"You might be able to alter it into something," she said. "I don't want more than $5 for this piece of junk."

Aunt Märta's Chest of Drawers

Ninety percent of our house is decorated with secondhand goods. Aunt Märta's old belongings, family heirlooms, and flea market finds. Things I found in junk shops and objects I swapped with friends. This motivates me to try and make my house beautiful with only limited resources. They were experts at this back in the olden days! Today, we try our best to imitate the look of that bygone era, inspired by Thomas Kinkade, *Pippi Longstocking,* and *Little House on the Prairie.*

One of my absolute favorite pieces of furniture came from Aunt Märta—my husband's aunt. She was creative and artistic, and even after she went blind she still made the most gorgeous laces. She also painted this chest of drawers—an entire dresser covered with painted roses. Her fingers must have been itching with creativity. At our house, Aunt Märta's dresser has the place of honor, and I keep my underwear and jewelry here.

You too can hand paint a dresser. The easiest way is to lay the dresser down flat and sketch the motif you'd like. Craft paint and a watercolor brush are good to use and a plate can be used to mix the palette. If you don't want to paint freehand, you can use the same decoration technique I used to scrapbook my closet (see page 26).

Jewelry Art

I never really understood why we keep jewelry in boxes hidden away in some dusty drawer! Jewelry is meant to be seen, and at my house, I love to spread it around and let it decorate the room.

Jewelry Tray

My retro jewelry looks a bit like small candy, and I usually have it lying around in pretty dishes. The tall, pressed glass trays shown below are made from old candlesticks and glass plates that I glued together, but it's also possible to combine narrow vases and little trays.

Instructions: Apply some glass adhesive around the top of the candlestick, and place the bottom of the plate in the center. Let dry. It's really that simple.

Brooch Board

My brooch board is a cute decoration and it keeps track of all my brooches.

Instructions: Remove the cardboard backing of a picture frame and place it on the fabric that you want to dress the frame with. Using the board as a stencil, trace along the edges and cut out the fabric. Then, clamp the fabric on to the backside of the frame with a staple gun. The fabric must be stretched properly. Pin the brooches on the fabric, and hang the "brooch board" on the wall.

> **WHAT YOU NEED:**
> - picture frame, with the glass removed
> - fabric
> - staple gun

TIP!

. . . .

- At flea markets you can find the best jewelry bargains by far! Look for old brooches, and if you're really lucky you might be able to dig up a vintage, cameo brooch from the $1 box.
- A nice alternative to the jewelry dish is to create a jewelry tree. Find a sturdy birch stick that has many branches and place it in a vase. Then just drape beautiful necklaces on the branches.

Clean Greener

There's no need to use horrible chemicals and detergents when cleaning. In our home, we use soft soap, vinegar, baking soda, and a dash of detergent. With this, you can manage everything. But one thing I absolutely don't want to be without is flaxseed oil soft soap. This is a magical product—fatter than regular soap and incredibly useful! Sometimes we wash linens and sheets in flaxseed oil soft soap, and afterward they smell like a summer meadow. An impulse-buy dress from the flea market had yellow stains under the arms that wouldn't go away in the laundry. I rubbed the armholes with soft soap and let it work for a few hours; when I rinsed it off, the dress was perfect. Dirty dogs and paint brushes become clean with soft soap, rusty fittings and keys will no longer be tarnished after a day in soft soap, and a little soft soap instead of liquid hand soap is good for your hands as it also moisturizes. I know people who even wash their hair with flaxseed oil soft soap!

Refurbish an Ironing Board

At our house, as soon as we put away the ironing board we need it again. So, we usually just leave it out. But this is no big deal, since it has such a lovely cover.

WHAT YOU NEED:

- cotton fabric, about 55 inches long × 30 inches wide
- elastic band

Instructions: Place the fabric on a table with the wrong side up. Lay the flat side of the ironing board down on top of the fabric. Trace the outline of the board on the fabric like a stencil. Draw another outline 1 ¼ inches around the first line. Cut the fabric out along the outer margin and zigzag stitch the edges.

Fold and pin approximately half an inch along the fabric edge. Sew the fold with a straight stitch, but leave an opening of half an inch where the elastic band can be pulled through. Pull the ribbon through the channel. Put the cover over the board and tighten the band in the channel at the bottom of the board so that the fabric is secured. Tie the strap so that it fits snugly.

Ironing Water

Ironing water is a real luxury that leaves a delightful fragrance in the linen cupboard.

Instructions: Dissolve the oil in the alcohol overnight. Pour the water into a bottle and add in the oil blend. Shake vigorously. Add a few drops of the "ironing water" to a spray bottle filled with water, or add a few drops directly to the iron's water compartment.

WHAT YOU NEED:

- 15 drops of essential oil
- a few drops of rubbing alcohol
- ⅛ cup distilled water

In Good Taste?

Bright, fresh, and white. A natural color palette. White is zero, the starting position—it's flawless. A sign of good taste. Or maybe just a lack of imagination?

I've always thought it sounds awkward when people claim they love natural colors and then decorate in white and beige. A common misconception in interior design is that it's easiest to decorate with a white base—advice regularly given to the novice decorator. I would suggest the opposite. A white base is extremely demanding. It's difficult to get a completely white home to feel cozy, even with comfortable furniture, beautiful fabrics, and ambitious lighting. The result is often sterile and flat. Patterned wallpaper, however, gives the feeling that a room is lived in. With really nice wallpaper, you can have old, vintage furniture. The wallpaper does the job. Even those who are afraid to wallpaper an entire room might instead focus on one or two walls. Or why not wallpaper the ceiling?

Of course, I love to mismatch colors and patterns. Somehow it feels soothing to the eye. I love plaid with polka dots and stripes with floral print. It meshes so well! Before, I used to be embarrassed when classy types stepped into my home. I was ashamed of my colorful mismatching of patterns. In the company of the minimalist, I became the silly, giggly over-decorated woman at the somber party: tasteless and way over the top! So hopelessly far from the low-key Scandinavian style that is the ideal of good taste. It was a sad feeling. Decorating shouldn't be woeful; it should be life affirming. So I decided to anticipate the frowns and proudly declare that I love to decorate with natural colors—red as geraniums, pink as fireweed, and popping green as the leaves in spring. And as for decorations, moderation is too little and too much is never enough. In my opinion, my honored guests, good taste can go screw itself.

Children's Room

Decorating a child's room is a decorator's dream. In the kids' room you can let your creativity free; colors that we otherwise don't dare use get plenty of free rein and flair.

Our son's room is a nice space in two ways: as a playroom and with a small alcove for the crib. Most of the stuff for this room was inherited or purchased at flea markets. Children's stuff is great to buy secondhand. And baby clothes that are a little worn from washing out are quite comfortable for the sensitive tykes.

Polka Dots and Blazing Yellow

Our son's room is located in the north of the house, so blazing yellow was an obvious color choice. I found the '60s vinyl wallpaper at a flea market. Three rolls for $10—as found! The wallpaper was not enough for the entire room, so the rest had to be white. A liter of yellow paint was left over from the kitchen renovation, so I used that to paint the doorframe and tie the two rooms together. That type of luck—when you just take what you have at home and combine it in a new way—gives me goosebumps!

Polka Dot Lamp

The polka dot lamp in my son Bertil's room was a boring thing from Ikea that I vintage pimped. It's easy to upholster fabric lampshades.

WHAT YOU NEED:

- lampshade
- fabric
- fabric glue

Instructions: Drape the fabric you want to use around the lampshade. Attach it first with clothespins to make sure it actually reaches all the way around. Cut any excess fabric, leaving a few inches on the top and bottom. Put fabric glue on the inside of the lampshade—along the top and bottom—and fold the fabric over the edges. Press firmly. Tighten the fabric around the shade. Hold the fabric in place with clothespins and let the glue dry. When glue has dried, you can pimp the lamp with pearls, lace, or pins. You can also decorate the fabric with fabric paint. I put some adhesive trim on the bottom.

Wallpaper Tips

- Dare to choose a pattern! Especially for the children's room, as pattern better hides marks and crayon streaks.
- Plain white wallpaper requires perfect prep work. Even a measly hair trapped under the wallpaper will appear as a thick rope. With bold wallpaper, the foundation is less important. Guess why older houses so often have patterned wallpaper!
- The first sheet is the trickiest to get straight. Use a spirit level.
- Make sure to have a good table to cut wallpaper on. And a sharp utility knife is a must.
- If you're unsure how to put up wallpaper, select the ones called Easy Up wallpaper. It requires you to apply the glue paste on the wall instead of the wallpaper.

Decorations, Junk, and More

If you're like me and love small trinkets and junk, it can easily begin to feel a bit messy at home. To avoid this, cluster your knickknacks in mini-installations. It soothes the eye and eases the dusting. Organize your mini-installations by themes: translucent glass gadgets, small porcelain animals, geranium cuttings, odd coffee cups, and so on. Place them in odd numbers—three or five candlesticks, rather than two and four. Window ledges don't have to be crowded with flowers. Group some trinkets on one side of the ledge, and put a beautiful vase at the other end. It's the negative space between them that makes them visible. The result is almost like an art exhibition.

Toys to Keep an Eye Out For at the Flea Market
- Wooden Brio toys
- Antique tin toys
- Smurfs (worth a fortune among collectors)
- Duplo and Lego, which can be expensive to buy new

Bean Bags

All small children love bean bags. Older kids do, too. All you need is a few handfuls of mung beans and fabric. Just be careful that the little ones don't swallow the beans.

Instructions: Cut two pieces of fabric 6 × 6 inches. Place their right sides against each other and pin along the edges. Sew around the edges with a straight stitch, but leave a gap of an inch. Turn the bag right-side-out and, using a funnel, fill it with beans. I usually fill them to about four-fifths full, so that the bags are cuddly and malleable. Then, hand sew the opening closed.

Textile Art

Textile art is as much art as any precious paintings, and in Bertil's room hang some of the the world's finest crafts in the shape of a wall hanging and a quilted blanket.

Fairy God Mother Wall Hanging

My mom's friends sewed the pretty wall hanging above the crib for her when she was pregnant. They each made one square with a familiar storybook motif. It was a super thoughtful gift that was displayed during my childhood, and now it's with my son.

Patchwork

Sewing a quilt may seem difficult, but it's actually quite simple if you do careful groundwork. Remember to wash all fabrics first, so they'll have shrunk completely before they are joined together. For this blanket, I used squares measuring 6 × 6 inches (15 × 15 cm). It's seven squares long and five squares wide. Instead of stuffing, I chose to attach a thicker lining fabric to the back.

Instructions: Cut thirty-five 7 × 7-inch (17 × 17 cm) squares (an inch for seam allowance) and lay them out on the floor in the desired pattern. Pin together the squares of the first stack, right sides together, to form a long strip. Sew together with a straight stitch. Repeat for all five stacks. Then put strip number one edge to edge with strip number two, right sides together. Pin the strips and sew with a straight stitch along the long side. Unfold and place strip number two on top of strip number three. Pin and sew strips with a straight stitch along the long side. Repeat with all the strips until they stick together as a quilt.

Place the quilt with the wrong side up, and press the seam allowances with an iron so that it is flat and smooth. Then place together the patchwork and the lining that has been cut to fit the blanket (30 × 40 in [75 × 105 cm]). Pin them with right sides together. Sew with a straight stitch around the quilt, about half an inch (1 cm) from the edge. Leave a space on the short side so that the quilt can be reversed. Press the seam allowances on the wrong side so they become flat and smooth. Turn the blanket right side out and close the opening on the short side.

Regarding Flea Markets

When brand new furniture can be bought for a pittance is there any real reason to save the old stuff? Well, what happens to originality when everyone buys their wardrobe from H&M and their furniture from IKEA? I think it's crazy to turn down Grandma and Grandpa's carefully crafted wooden chairs in favor of mass-produced products that start to wobble after just a year.

The clothing and furniture produced in Sweden at the end of the '60s was of phenomenal quality. The pieces were made to last, and they still do today. It's perhaps the single most important reason for buying used: You get more for your money than if you buy new. Clothing and furniture have never been more affordable than they are now. Nor have they been more expensive, as we truly get what we pay for. If you buy newly produced shoes for $30, you can be one hundred percent sure that someone along the way was taken advantage of or exploited. Today, there are no new shoes that are that cheap and still ethically made and of good quality. For instance, today you can only achieve the quality of a flea market bargain dress from the '50s by going to a tailor and getting something custom made.

I fear that we're annihilating our heritage in the rush to constantly consume what's new and modern. Therefore, I'm happy to see the counter-trend that exists right now, where people are running to garage sales and auctions like never before. Bidding on online auction sites, swapping clothes, altering, and changing what's already in their homes. It gives me hope!

Nothing makes my heart pound like a really good flea market. I sneak around on shaky legs and examine the shelves with greedy eyes. Nothing escapes me. I clutch my findings to my chest, as if they were a newborn baby. Greed is central. The feeling of making the find of my life is what drives me. I actually think it's the treasure hunt that's so amazing, not the treasure itself. The feeling of not being able to predict what you might find. Somewhere, at a flea market at the world's end, there's a treasure so great that the imagination cannot conceive of it. It may be a flashy dress, an elite coffee powder measure, or a plate with an unusual pattern. It may seem insignificant to someone else, but it's a treasure to me. Because I was the one who found it!

This is why I think antique stores and well-stocked vintage shops feel a bit like cheating. It's too easy. The treasure hunt is no longer exciting when someone else has done the work for me (and already gotten the best bargains). No, the ideal flea market is located in a lonely road in the middle of nowhere. Far from the city hipsters, stylists, and fashionistas. I want to be the only one making discoveries, like the greedy treasure hunter I am. And above all, I want to brag about the bargains afterward, so people's faces turn visibly green with envy. "Look what a wonderful little teapot I found . . . antique porcelain, only $1 at some out of the way flea market I almost drove past. . . . Take you there? Oh, no, I would never be able to find my way back, I'm afraid."

It's difficult not to constantly shop for something new. My best trick for reducing this craving is to simply stop going to stores. I avoid running around town, because I know that I most certainly will find something I'll believe that I need. Instead, I draw inspiration from vintage bloggers and I shop till I drop at flea markets if the longing for a bargain becomes unbearable. Sure, it's limiting. But from limitation, creativity is born. Necessity is the mother of all invention. At the flea market, I'm challenged to think one step further and in an innovative way, because it's not easy to decorate beautifully with old junk. But it is fun. And very satisfying.

The Commandments of Flea Markets

- Locate current garage sales in the local newspaper's weekend editions.
- Cash is king! Always bring cash and small change.
- Be there on time. The best bargains go first.
- Shop with your body. In secondhand shops, you won't be handed products. You'll have to lift, dig, twist, and turn. And don't worry about germs.
- Bring a folding ruler and have important dimensions jotted down. This helps avoid taking home a linen closet only to discover that you can't get it through the front door.
- Ask around. Many flea markets and antique shops buy estates—they tend be able to carve out everything from cast iron bathtubs to pewter candlesticks or porcelain. Moreover, they always have some goodies hidden. If you're friendly with an antique dealer, then you're in luck.
- Are you going to a secondhand shop for clothing? Dress in layers, with outer clothes that are easy to take off. Often there are no fitting rooms.
- Shopping for clothing is a challenge at flea markets. I scan for fun patterns and different textures. Perhaps an odd collar peeks out.
- Don't check the sizing label; they're rarely accurate. Always try on the garments. They often fit a bit haphazardly, and it's difficult to determine whether garments will fit right on the body.
- What if it has stains and odors, but is otherwise fine? Don't despair. See my tricks to the right.
- Always bargain for the price (unless the money goes to charitable causes).
- Don't look for anything in particular. The best bargains are found by accident.

How Do You Bargain?

I usually walk up to the checkout, throw up the treasure, and with a charming smile say: "What do you want for this?" The fact that there is already a price tag doesn't matter. If they tell you the same price as stated on the tag, I say, "No, no, you can do better than that!" And they always tend to be able to.

If I've found many goodies, I'll put them together in a pile and say, "Give me a good price on this, and I'll buy everything." It always works.

Freshen Up Flea Market Clothes

Musty odor in clothing and shoes can be removed with vinegar. Add two teaspoons of vinegar to a water-filled spray bottle. Spray the inside and outside of the garments and let them hang up to air and dry overnight. Or, hang the musty clothes in a closet and put a plate with vinegar on the closet floor. Let it stand for a few days and then air the garment out.

Flaxseed oil soft soap is another amazing natural product. For rust stains on textiles and ingrained yellow spots under sleeves, it is absolutely superb. Rub the stain with the soft soap and leave for a few hours. Rinse and repeat as necessary.

Lastly, we have gall soap—the catcher in the rye when nothing works. Order it online and use on any stubborn stain. It's extra effective for grease stains.

Kitchen

Updating a kitchen is probably one of the hardest home renovations you can do, and if I had any romantic notions about home renovation, they disappeared then and there. I learned that the cliché "the kitchen is the heart of the home" is used for a reason—without a kitchen, you feel homeless. During our kitchen renovation, life became a mess.

We wanted to replace the water-damaged '80s kitchen with a kitchen that had an older style but modern function, and we wanted cupboards that used the full height of the wall, with cupboards all the way up. Our minimal budget meant that a brand new "catalogue kitchen" was out of the picture. But where would we get the kitchen we wanted at a price we could afford? My brother had the idea to advertise for it on my blog, and can you believe it?—we found it! A reader's grandmother had an original '50s-era kitchen that was about to be thrown out. We snagged it.

We kept the original color of the cupboards—light green doors and blazing yellow interiors. We dressed the walls with a wallpaper called "Ruth" from Sandberg wallpaper. We bought a new countertop with the classic '50s pattern "VirrVarr." Both the dishwasher and the refrigerator are built into the existing cabinets and are effectively hidden.

In with the Old, Out with the New

Cheap porcelain will rattle and scrape when used, so much so that it'll grate on your ears when you're supposed to be enjoying your meal. Glazed British porcelain, on the other hand . . . it really sings when you eat off it. It doesn't matter if the porcelain on the table is mismatched or belongs to a bunch of different sets. On the contrary, I think it looks charming.

Pimped-Out Porcelain
Self-adhesive porcelain plastic is an ideal way to pimp boring porcelain, and you can order it online in a variety of colors. I did both the cute tea set and the carnival-striped plates by hand, without a template.

Instructions: Wash the porcelain plate carefully and wipe it dry. Measure the radius of the plate and cut triangles of porcelain plastic to be a few inches longer than the radius. Soak the strips so that the backing paper comes off. Then, paste the triangles with the tip at the middle of the plate and the base to the edge. Iron the strips on so that all the bubbles disappear. Dry the plate after attaching each strip so that it's completely dry; this way the plastic will attach better. Allow the plate to cure in an oven for 30 minutes at 350 degrees Fahrenheit, or as described on the package. Of course, this also works for making fun designs by hand.

Scrapbooked Junk Tray

Pimp a flea market find with a scrapbooking technique.

Instructions: Place the tray on the scrapbook paper or wallpaper, and trace along the outer edge with a pencil. Cut out the paper along the markings. Apply wallpaper paste generously to the back of the paper, and let it swell for a minute. Place the paper on the tray, and flatten out any air bubbles with your hand. Keep stroking until the glue has dried so that the paper stays in place. Apply a translucent lacquer to the surface. Let dry and apply another coat of lacquer. Repeat 1–2 times.

WHAT YOU NEED:

- kitchen tray in unpolished wood
- scrapbook paper or wallpaper
- wallpaper paste
- translucent lacquer
- brush

Sew an Apron from a Kitchen Towel

A tea towel easily can be transformed into an adorable apron. All you need is a kitchen towel in a larger size and a pretty tie.

Instructions: Cut two bands from a matching fabric, approximately 27 inches (70 cm) long. Pin the straps onto the wrong side on the short sides of the towel. Sew the bands with a straight stitch and presto! It's done.

Coffee Cup Candle

It's easy and fun to cast new candles from old wax stubs. All you need is cotton yarn for the wick and a mold to make the candles in. I used old coffee cups as molds. If you don't have any burned down candles, you can get candle wax at craft stores.

Instructions: Cut away any burned wicks from the candle stumps to keep black ash out of the candle wax. Heat a pot of water on low—don't boil. Note: Be sure to keep the stove fan off! Place a stainless steel bowl in the saucepan and add the candle stumps. The candles will start to melt. Take care that it doesn't overheat.

Trim the wicks of cotton yarn. They should be long enough that they reach to the bottom of the coffee cup, and preferably about 2 inches (5 cm) extra. Tie each wick to the center of a pencil, and then dip the wicks into the melted wax. They will become rigid and straight. Place the pencil straight over the coffee cup and center the wick in the cup. The pencil will ensure that the wick stays straight. Then pour the wax into the cup. After a couple of hours the wax will solidify, and you can add more if need be. Let the wax harden for a few more hours. Cut the wick from the pencil before you light the candle.

WHAT YOU NEED:

- cotton yarn to make a wick
- coffee cups or any other mold to make the candles in
- candle wax or old candle stubs

Almond Sponge Cake

I love Swedish almond tarts, but they're so much trouble to bake. Instead, I make a sponge cake that tastes like an almond tart. They're just as good, but so much easier.

You need:

3 eggs
1 ¼ cups (300 ml) granulated sugar
½ cup (100 ml) boiling water
1 tsp bitter almond oil
1 ¼ cups (300 ml) flour
1 ½ tsp baking powder

Glaze:

¾ cup (200 ml) powdered sugar
1 tbsp water
1 tbsp lemon juice

Instructions: Preheat oven to 400 degrees Fahrenheit (200 degrees Celcius).

Beat the eggs and sugar until fluffy. Add the hot water and bitter almond oil and whisk some more.

Combine the flour and baking powder in a bowl, and carefully tip the flour mixture into the egg mixture.

Pour the batter into a greased oven-safe Bundt pan, and bake at the bottom of the oven for about 30 minutes. Remove the cake from the mold and let cool.

Mix ingredients for the icing to a smooth cream, and drizzle it over the cake when cool. Irresistible!

String Shelves

The string shelf is an ingenious invention, but try to put one up on your own and it can end with a crash. At least four hands are recommended for this project—and high spirits! On my string shelves, cookbooks mingle with fancy tins, teapots, and other objects that make me happy to look at. On the little white shelf below, I store sprinkles and brightly colored cake decorations.

My Best Tips for Contemporary Refurbishment
- Old kitchens are often for sale online, and you can find old drawer-handles and hardware that will spice up newer drawers.
- Online websites are excellent sources of inspiration for contemporary house renovation and repair.
- Study period movies for true inspiration. When we renovated the kitchen, I studied old Swedish movies by Astrid Lindgren. They have great examples of authentic '40s and '50s kitchens—not some kitschy pastiche.

Lovely Lights

One of our best investments during the renovation is the woodstove in the kitchen. The house had one when it was built, but it was thrown out in the '70s. Now it's been reinstalled, and on chilly days we make fires that make the boiler glow red. But what I like most about it are the smells and sounds of burning birch wood. It's unbeatable! But if you're not fortunate enough to have a fireplace at home, candles make a really good substitute. I love candles, and I love to put lanterns all over the house.

Rustic Candleholder

A candleholder made from a piece of wood is a rustic piece that's beautiful in its simplicity. But don't leave it unattended and be sure to use self-extinguishing candles!

Instructions: Pick a beautiful log or piece of wood that will lay steady on the table—it's vital that it doesn't wobble. Nail down 5 nails, 2 inches (5 cm) long, at the desired distance from each other. Allow approximately one inch (2 cm) of each nail to stick up out of the wood and then snip off the head with pliers. Make sure they're straight. Carefully lower the self-extinguishing candles onto the nails.

Paupers' Sconce

Cute wall sconces are easy to make from old-fashioned Christmas tree lights and jar lids.

Instructions: Using a hammer and nail, make a hole in the jar lid for hanging. Fix a nail in the wall where you want your sconce to hang, and then hook the jar lid onto the nail; the top of the lid should be facing the wall. Then fix the Christmas tree candleholder in the rim of the jar lid, and place the candle in the holder.

WHAT YOU NEED:

- 1 jar lid
- 1 holder for Christmas tree lights
- 1 small Christmas tree light

Enamel Lamp

Enamel bowls and zinc buckets are excellent to make lamps out of. I bought this little tub for a dollar, and it took ten minutes to turn into a lamp. In other words, it is really easy if you know how to install a plug. Ask for help from an electrician if you're uncertain—they can fix it in no time!

Instructions: Turn the bucket upside down. Measure and mark the center point of the bottom with a cross. Be sure to measure accurately, otherwise the light will hang crooked. Drive the nail down on the mark to make a hole. To stop the nail from slipping around, you can fix it in place with freezer tape. Place a screwdriver in the hole, and hammer it down so that the hole extends. Disassemble the plug and release the cord. Thread the cord through the hole, and then reinstall the plug. Now the lamp is ready to use.

WHAT YOU NEED:

- enamel or metal bucket
- lamp holders
- large nail
- screwdriver
- hammer
- freezer tape
- tape measure

Vintage Girls' Books

Vintage girls' books usually have really nice covers and they're a great way to pimp notebooks.

Instructions: Carefully cut away the interior of the book with a utility knife so that only the cover remains. Cut an existing notepad so that it fits the book's dimensions. Use a staple gun to attach the notepad to the book cover. Or thread a string through the center of the notebook and tie at the spine. You can fasten this with a few stitches.

Lavender Biscuits

Lavender is a lovely herb that has no limits to its usefulness! In the linen closet, it scares away pests, and when used in cakes and pastries it's perfect for satisfying a sweet tooth. These biscuits are summer for me.

You Need:
7 tbsp (100 g) butter
2 tsp dried lavender
2 eggs
½ cup (150 ml) muscovado sugar
1 ¾ cups (400 ml) flour
½ cup (100 ml) whole grain spelt
1 ½ tsp baking powder
¾ cup (200 ml) whole almonds

Instructions: Preheat the oven to 350 degrees Fahrenheit (175 degrees Celcius).

Over low heat, melt the butter with the lavender. Allow to cool. Pour the melted butter into a large bowl and stir in the eggs.

Mix the dry ingredients together with the almonds. Add the flour mixture to the egg and butter mixture, and stir into a dough.

Shape the dough into three lengths and place them on a sheet with parchment paper. Bake in the center rack of the oven for about 25 minutes. Remove the lengths from the oven and reduce the temperature to 250 degrees Fahrenheit (125 degrees Celcius). Cut the lengths into ½-inch (1 cm) thick slices and return them to the oven for about 12 minutes. Turn off the oven and let the biscuits dry in the residual heat until the oven has cooled.

My Favorite Cookies
• Swedish Dream Cookies
• Russian Tea Cakes
• Raspberry Thumbprint Cookies

I decorated this tray with
scrapbook paper. See page 65.

Living Room

The living room is a space to socialize and relax. Here, I catch up with friends or watch movies while curled up on the couch. But it's also one of the most difficult rooms to furnish and it can be as big a source of frustration as it is of relaxation. Technology is the culprit. Often, you have a television to work around and most likely a music system as well. If you're really lucky (unlucky?), you may also have a monster piano getting in the way. Add a twenty-foot power cord, and the situation becomes untenable!

Our living room is furnished for socializing. A good tip is to arrange the furniture in the middle of the room instead of pushing it up against the walls, which might be your first inclination. This makes it airier and much more inviting. And of course you need lots of pillows on the couch! Forget everything you've heard about less being more!

My father-in-law built the bookcase in the living room for us. It's a pretty and roomy piece that reaches up to the ceiling—the maximum utilization of space.

I bought the little star-patterned radio at a department store and painted it yellow with ordinary wall paint. The stars are actually stickers that I attached when the paint dried. And if I get tired of looking at it, I can easily paint it again.

Green Is Good

Few things make the house more homey than living plants. They make you feel happy and energized, and they purify the air and provide a better indoor climate. If you don't have a green thumb, you'll usually be told to go for easy options like cacti, Mother-in-Law's Tongue, and Zanzibar Gem. But ouch! Who wants to take care of such prickly plants? They give you no affection. Focus instead on lush, happy, and nice flowers—even if you don't have a green touch. I've found that people only take good care of things that they appreciate and enjoy. Myself, I love geraniums. Sometimes I forget to water them for weeks, but they remain healthy and in bloom. You can easily increase their number by breaking off a twig and putting it into a pot with soil. With some nutrients and plenty of sun, they'll bloom nicely from March to December.

They are popularly called the poor man's roses, but I think this undervalues the geranium. It's not only a beautiful plant, but it also smells delightful. Try Mårbacka Geraniums for a rural feel.

Five Beautiful Flowers That Like to Survive
- Christmas Cactus
- Saint Paulia
- Orchid
- Kalanchoe
- Impatiens

Planting in Shoes
My old worn out work shoes are covered with splashes of paint—something that is actually really beautiful! I filled these shoes with matching spring onions and gave them new life (literally!). Bulbs are perfect for this, as they don't require too much water and don't need to be placed in conventional well-draining pots. Just remember to place them in the sunshine. If you care for the shoes, you can put the plants in a small plastic bag.

Monica Zetterlund and Other Wonderful Tunes

Our speakers from the '70s had impeccable sound, but unfortunately, they were pretty hideous. The fabric on the removable fronts had grown yellowed and cracked—so I replaced it with beautiful lace.

I also pimped the rice-paper ceiling lamp with old plastic flowers.

My Favorite Songs, Top 5
- "The Last Lass" by Monica Zetterlund
- "Blue Mountains" by Tomas Andersson Wij
- "Wishin' and Hopin'" by Dusty Springfield
- "There's Hope" by India Arie
- "Foolish Games" by Jewel

Pimped Speakers
Pimping speakers is simple—just make sure the fabric's not too tight across the speakers, as that will affect sound quality.

Instructions: Remove the frames on the front of the speakers and untuck the existing fabric. Lay the discarded fabric on the back of the new fabric, and trace the edges with a pencil. Cut the new fabric along the markings. Place the frames on the wrong side of the fabric and stretch the fabric around the edges of the frame. Then attach the fabric to the backs of the frames with a staple gun.

> **WHAT YOU NEED:**
> - lace or another sheer fabric
> - staple gun

Flower Ball
A boring rice-paper lamp got new life when I pimped it with plastic flowers. A bit fiddly, maybe, but it's unique!

Instructions: Disassemble a few bouquets of plastic flowers, and remove the hard, protruding plastic pieces that might destroy the rice lamp. Using a glue gun, distribute small dots of glue around the lamp. Press the flowers onto the glue and let dry. The finished lamp will be very fragile because of the added weight and should be handled with care.

> **WHAT YOU NEED:**
> - plastic flowers
> - rice lamp
> - glue gun

Grandma Beda's Invite Jar

As a child, when I visited my grandma, the first thing I did was rush to the living room to clear out the "invite jar." You don't know what an invite jar is? You've really missed out! An invite jar is a candy jar on display for guests to serve themselves. Grandma Beda had a green one made of bubbly glass. I was constantly over there, digging in, and stuffing my cheeks full of caramel beans. Grandma was never stingy with the candy.

The invite jar symbolizes the comforts of home and security, and one of the very first things I bought when I left home was my very own candy jar. Every time I see it I think of my grandmother. Robust and sweet and full of candy—just like the generous way she filled up the jar. To prevent my jar from suffering the same fate, I fill it with just enough tasty candy. Not so tasty that it's impossible for me to resist, but still yummy enough that guests will be delighted to be invited to eat. That's the candy jar in a nutshell. The jar should be placed prominently in the kitchen or living room, so guests feel free to help themselves. If you think they're taking too much, keep quiet—the invite jar is not conditional.

The Best Candy for an Invite Jar

- Peppermint candy
- Chocolate covered raisins
- Werther's Original
- Jelly beans
- Caramels

Twig Lantern

I made this little twig lantern from a tealight cup and birch twigs. It is easiest if the tealight cup is fairly straight in shape.

Instructions: Snip the twigs to the same length as the height of the lantern. Birch twigs work nicely. Put a rubber band around the tea light cup and insert the twigs under the band. When the whole cup is covered, tie a pretty string around the sticks tightly. Once it's properly fastened, you can cut off the rubber band.

Birch Bark Lantern

Birch bark is incredibly beautiful, and I usually take advantage of some of the bark before the wood goes into the fire.

Instructions: Soak the birch bark overnight so that it becomes soft and pliable. Cut the birch bark into the desired size and wrap it around a candle cup. Secure it with a rubber band and let it dry. Tie a neat piece of string around the bark. When it sits firmly, cut off the rubber band.

Little Things—Big Difference

Garland of Rowan Berries

Pierce each rowan berry with a needle, and thread them onto a string—like you would when making a beaded necklace—and presto! You have a nifty berry garland. I usually make several short berry garlands that I then tie together. This way, if the thread breaks, you won't have to redo everything. Hang the garland to dry. Strong cotton thread is best!

Atlas Pennant

This fun pennant was super easy to make. I cut out large triangles from an atlas and made two holes a short distance apart at the base of each triangle. Then, I threaded some string through the holes. Done!

Animal Frame

I painted an ugly old pinewood frame from the flea market black and vintage pimped it with plastic toys.

Instructions: Wipe the frame and plastic animals with a cloth and a little detergent. Paint the frame and the animals with 2–3 layers of water-based paint. Let them dry. Once you've found the best place for the animal toys, dab some glue on their feet and press them onto the frame. Hold them steady with your hand until the glue has dried.

WHAT YOU NEED:

- frame
- plastic animals
- water-based paint
- brush
- superglue

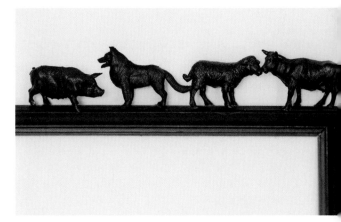

Recesses

Hallways, staircases, nooks, and crannies are what give a house its character. Perhaps this is why old houses are so much more fun than new ones? They're usually full of out-of-the-way nooks—perfect for a reading area, a children's hideout, or a small desk. New houses, however, are like large gymnasiums where no one can hide and nothing can be kept a little secret. Many people renovate and remove these nooks because they're perceived as impractical. Personally, I think just the opposite. With a little creativity, these odd places can be turned into storage spaces where you can hide winter clothes, pantry items, toys, and DVDs—things you might otherwise never know where to put. So consider carefully before knocking out the walls for a more open floor plan. You don't realize how empty it looks until it's too late!

Beloved Office

A woman must have a room of her own, said Virginia Woolf, and she knew what she was talking about. Having your own corner—even if it's cramped—is critical for creativity. If your sewing machine is out, threaded, and ready, and if the paint cans are prepped on the shelves—the steps between thought and action are few. But if you have to begin by cleaning up mess and preparing your space, you'll never seem ready to get started. So unnecessary!

In my office, crafts are always around. Here the sewing machine mixes with paint cans, fabric remnants, and paper scraps. I hoard everything; a seemingly insignificant scrap of fabric might be transformed into a fancy bow on a birthday present. What's good about having it all around me is that I actually remember to use it. The bad thing is that it attracts a lot of dust. You'll simply have to choose: dusty and creative, or dust free and unimaginative?

Tray Bulletin Board
A large metal tray makes a great bulletin board. Make a hole in it with a nail and hook it up on the wall, or hang it with tag tape.

Orderliness

Jar Shelf

The jar shelf is an ingenious invention for maximizing space.

Instructions: Clean the jars and caps firmly. Then place the shelf upside down and lay down the jar lids, with the tops toward the shelf, at the desired distance from each other. Attach the lids to the shelf with a strong staple gun or with a screw and a screwdriver. Turn the shelf over and screw the jars into the lids.

TIP!
....
When I have bottles with labels that don't want to come off, I soak them for few hours and then brush them with rapeseed oil. Then I use the back of a dish brush to scrape off the remaining glue.

Preserves and Bottles

Tin cans and odd bottles get new lives as vases, candleholders, and penholders. Colorful, convenient, and cheap!

WHAT YOU NEED:

- glass jars with lids
- shelves
- staple gun

Pincushion Wristband

A pincushion that is secured to the wrist is very convenient when sewing. Here I simply sewed a satin ribbon onto an existing pincushion. It's just as practical, but far less pretty, if you attach a rubber band to the pincushion.

Pincushion from an Old Sardine Can

A more conventional but still unique pincushion is easily made with an old sardine can.

Instructions: Cut a piece of fabric that is as long as the sardine can but twice as wide. Fold the fabric twice, right sides together. Pin along the edges and sew it together, either by sewing machine or by hand, but leave a small opening. Turn the fabric and fill it with batting. Sew the opening closed by hand and then press the fabric pad into the can. The metal edges keep the cushion in place!

> **WHAT YOU NEED:**
>
> - an empty and clean sardine can
> - a piece of cloth
> - batting for padding

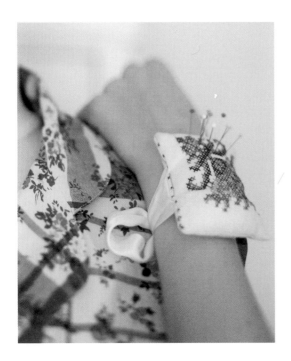

The World's Best Office

A Different Bulletin Board

I was looking for a bulletin board when I found this rusty plate in a corner of the garden. With the help of some magnets, it became a practical and unique bulletin board. If you're worried about damaging the surface behind, you can paint the plate with a transparent lacquer to prevent rust stains. I just leaned the board against the wall, but you can also hang it with nails. Just makes some small holes in the plate and hook it up. If you're not lucky enough to find an appropriate sheet in your garden, you can buy a sheet of metal for about ten dollars. That way you can get the dimensions you want.

Wall Atlas

As a kid, I had a writing desk pad that looked like a world map, and I would sit in front of it for long hours and dream myself away to distant lands. I'm still fond of maps and old atlases, and you can do a lot of nice things with them. I wallpapered one wall in our house with pages from an old atlas. It's easy and all you need is a map, wallpaper paste, and a broad brush. If you're not into maps, then it works equally well with pages from books with graceful text. Try to wallpaper a little higgledy-piggledy—it'll look like a patchwork.

Instructions: Cut out map pages with a utility knife. Use a ruler along the edges so that the cuts are straight. Brush the wall with wallpaper paste, a little at a time so that the adhesive doesn't have time to dry. Then coat a thin layer of glue on the back of a map page. Stick the page on the wall and remove any bubbles by smoothing with your hand. It's important that the first map pages sit straight (use a spirit level), that way you'll have something to work from and the rest of the wallpapering becomes much easier. Check regularly that it's still straight.

Magnets

I made magnets shaped like letters from the magnetic plastic that can be purchased at craft stores. I first made a template on plain paper and traced it on the back of the magnetic resin. Then, I just cut along the markings using a utility knife. But it's also possible to cut out the letters with sharp scissors.

The Reading Corner in the Stairwell

The wicker chair in the stairwell is our dog Melker's favorite spot. Here, he snores comfortably. I found the armchair at a flea market and spray-painted it white. Generally I avoid spray paint because of the environmentally-cruel bottles, but wicker furniture is almost impossible to paint with a brush. I upholstered the cushion with remnants of a torn quilt. It was just enough for the cushion.

Frame Tray

Replace the motif in a pretty frame and use it instead as a snack tray! With beautiful wallpaper remnants, the frame gets a completely new look, and the glass protects against splashes and stains. Just make sure that the backside of the tray is made of wood and is securely riveted so that it holds the weight.

Books for a Rainy Day
- *Sense and Sensibility* by Jane Austen
- *Les Misérables* by Victor Hugo
- *Agnes Cecilia* by Maria Gripe
- *The Emperor of Portugallia* by Selma Lagerlöf

Clock of Jar Lids

In craft stores, you can find clock hands and clockwork, and by using these, you can turn most things into a clock. Like a jar lid, for example.

Instructions: Measure the center of the jar lid, mark it with a small "x," and punch a hole in that spot with a hammer and a nail. Install the clockwork and the hands according to the instructions on the packaging.

WHAT YOU NEED:
- jar lid
- hammer
- nail
- clock hands and clockwork

Sugar Box Bookshelves

I found these sugar boxes in a relative's attic. I love sugar boxes for their versatility. They work as a bedside table, flower boxes—so why not as bookshelves? Some boxes were tasked with holding books and magazines in my reading corner. They stand steady since I screwed straight through the bottom panel to attach them to the wall.

TIP!
. . . .
You can usually find sugar boxes at garage sales, although they've gone up in price over the last few years. A great budget alternative is fruit boxes from the grocery store. At Christmas, mandarins usually come in wooden boxes, and if you ask nicely, you can usually get a few.

Colorful Flower Pots

In my reading corner there are flower pots that I painted with a little leftover paint. They were cracked and discolored but were freshened up with a few strokes of the brush. Porcelain color is not necessary—I used regular lacquer paint. Fire red pots—I'm sure I'm the only one!

Coffee Patinated Picture of Leaves

Small leaves pinned up in a frame almost look like butterflies—beautiful but not as brutal. Beneath the leaves, I have written their Latin names in pretty writing. I painted the frame, which was originally pure white, with some coffee. You get the prettiest result by using a so-called box frame (a frame that has some distance between the base and the glass); this way the leaves don't get flattened.

Instructions: Dip a paintbrush into a cup of coffee and brush over the frame. Dab away any excess coffee with some paper towels and let dry. If you want to fix the patinate, paint it with translucent lacquer. Then attach the leaves to the board.

Upholstering Old Furniture

My mother was a master at upholstering furniture. I am not as good as she was, but I succeeded with my favorite chair, the ironing board, and the piano stool. People who are clearly prone to spilling croaked that I absolutely could not dress my armchair in regular cotton fabric and that I had to choose a fabric designed for furniture. You can go either way, in my opinion. Regular upholstery fabric is usually hopelessly boring, and if you're not planning on using the furniture excessively, a heavy cotton fabric works just fine.

I think the easiest way to upholster a piece of furniture is to rip off the old cloth and trace its outline onto a cheap cotton fabric. Then I usually try to attach cotton fabric around the seat to see if I have been thinking correctly. When everything is to my satisfaction, I remove the cheap fabric and trace its outer edges onto the new and pretty fabric I intend to use. An ambitious person will do all the stitching by hand. I, however, use a much simpler method. A stapler on the underside and upholstery tacks for all visible areas. Fabric glue is also good to have.

Considerations for the Amateur Upholsterer

• Choose a piece of furniture that is not too curvy. Straight lines are easiest to work with.

• The furniture must be intact and shouldn't have a sloping seat. To both replace the fabric and upholster the inside of the seat can be a bit difficult if you're a beginner.

• Select a fabric that doesn't have to be fitted according to its pattern. Alternatively, don't bother trying to fit the pattern.

• Start by upholstering a piece of furniture that you don't care about too much. In order to learn, you must dare to fail.

• Get the right tools before you begin. Scissors, needle, seam ripper, tape measure, pliers, staple gun for furniture, fabric glue, and a hammer are all good to have.

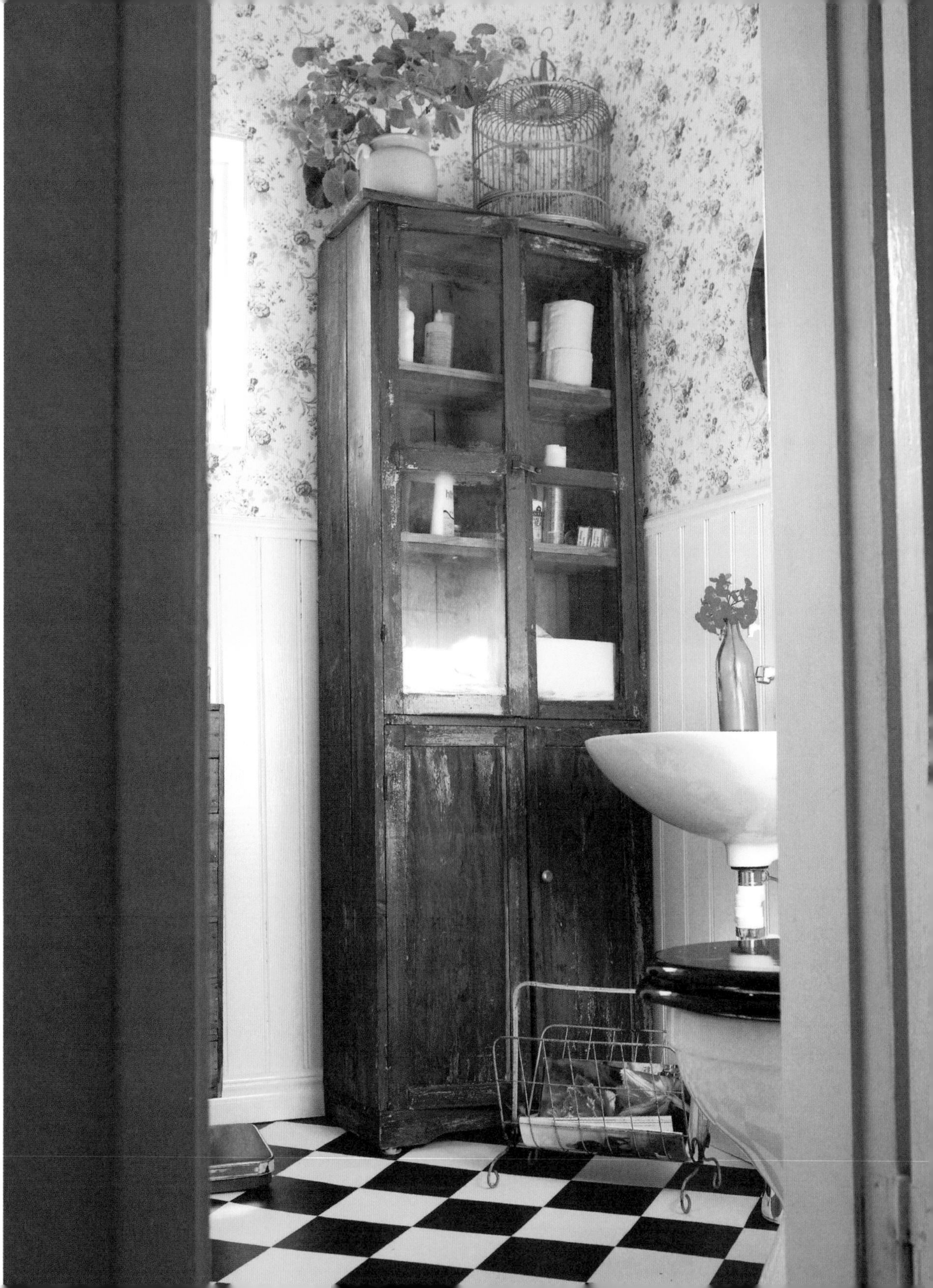

The Guest Bathroom

A stylish bathroom interior is almost impossible to find new. And if you want to buy something a little different, you have to sell your kids at auction just to be able to afford it! But who says there has to be bathroom furniture in the bathroom? I put in an old cabinet that I found for cheap at an antique shop and a matching dresser built from sugar boxes. It instantly became a lot more personal.

The old wooden paneling got to stay, and I painted it creamy white. Large, floral wallpaper with a vintage look went up on the wall. For the flooring, I have a black and white checkered vinyl mat. I chose to angle it so the squares form diamonds. It makes the room feel larger and gives it a '20s twist.

Since the sink and the toilet were flawless, I settled by only replacing the tap with a nicer, old-fashioned style and the toilet got a black Bakelite seat. Altogether, the cost of the bathroom renovation was less than $800.

The chest of drawers made from sugar boxes is ideal storage for all the small stuff found in a bathroom. The porcelain knobs on the boxes were also up-cycled—they were once used to mount electricity. A shrewd relative built this chest of drawers in the '40s. Talk about chic recycling!

Manufacturers That Make Great Retro Wallpaper

- Sandberg
- Intrade
- Sanderson
- Osborne & Little
- PiP Studio
- Boråstapeter

Hanging Flower Vase

Flowers in the bathroom are super luxurious. I hung the pressed glass flower vase from the towel rack with a loop of wire around the lip. You can also place a scented candle in the vase. Then, you'll have a lantern.

Can Lantern

Old cans can become beautiful with regular tea lights.

Instructions: Empty the can. Fill it with water, and place in the freezer. Remove the can, and use a hammer and a nail to make small holes in the can. The ice in the can prevents it from getting dented. Also make two small holes at the top at the rim, and secure the wire for hanging.

Antique Magazine Basket

I found the antique magazine basket in a relative's storage locker, and it keeps the bathroom reading material in order. I know there are people who shudder at the idea of reading on the toilet, but I can assure you that it's only on extremely rare occasions that someone actually reads with their butt.

TIP!

- Throw out the new bathroom mirror and instead, hang up a flea market find with a beautiful frame—the simplest and cheapest trick for a charming bathroom.
- Replace dull hooks with unique knobs and stubs.
- Opt for fun towels—a cheap trick that makes a big difference.
- Pictures in the bathroom make it even more homey.

The Dream of Having Your Own House

A castle in the south of France, a mansion in the Rhineland, or a grand yard by a murmuring river? I have dreamed many dreams about the house I would have. But what I finally bought was a stucco house from the '30s. Pretty ordinary—but at an extraordinary price! It cost about as much as twenty-one square feet in downtown Stockholm.

We all look for different things when we buy a house. Me, I kept an eye out for original windows, wooden floors, and extra high ceilings. If those things you want are available the rest will usually work out. When we bought our house, friends complained about how outdated it was. But where others saw a house with drafty windows, we saw a house with its charm intact. When a neighbor grimly remarked that the roof had never been replaced, I said, "Thank goodness!" We thought it was perfect that the house didn't have a modern bathroom—that way, we could build it old-fashioned straight away. No one had been there to destroy anything. I love the elements that are full of character and all the artful little nooks and recesses. If I wanted a house with an open design and easy-to-mop floors, I would have ordered it from a catalog. The floors creak and snap, the walls talk at night, and the smell of wood fills the kitchen when we light the fire—this is what is makes it so cozy. But my grandfather was concerned that we had chosen a primitive house—a man who had grown up with an outhouse and weeks of chopping wood for the winter and who found a heat pump to be the height of happiness. Who is so stupid to voluntarily opt out of triple glazing, a maintenance-free metal roof, and practical plastic mats?

Honestly, I am perfectly happy to chop wood. I'm not so sure that all this modern stuff really saves us time. Rather, I think we replace one task with another. We swapped wood chopping for trips to the gym. And quite frankly, a load of wood is a lot cheaper than a gym membership.

Seven Home Improvement Lessons

- Estimate how long it will take and then multiply by two. Then you get close to about 70 percent of the time it will actually take. And cost!

- Don't rush. I am terribly impatient, but I've discovered that the best ideas come when I have wandered and pondered for a while.

- Expect that it will be a hassle. Add a hefty hassle allowance to each step to avoid disappointment and frustration. It's like a seam allowance, but for renovation.

- Expect that any craftsmen you may need to call in will be busy. Book them some months in advance.

- If you're renovating an entire house, I think it makes sense to alternate between small and large projects. It is boring to replace heating systems, so after that you can do something simple and fun that energizes rather than enervates. Paint a wall, for example. Or sew new curtains for the kitchen.

- Ask family and friends for help. Most people have nothing against helping out for a few hours. Serve them a delicious meal in return.

Garden

Before I bought a house, my fingers were more pink than green. But now I've started shaping up. Sometimes I even think it's more fun to decorate the garden than the house, because the garden has a life of its own and its own free will. Additionally, I get a long winter break from any failures. My garden may be a bit rugged; I prefer overgrown bushes and a mess of flowerbeds to a crew-cut lawn and sparse rows of tulips.

I think the key to a pleasant garden is to relax and think of it as your living room. A place to hang out, cozy up, and have peaceful moments—not something to impress the neighbors.

I tend to plant seedlings in small pots made of newspaper. It's inexpensive, environmentally friendly,
and you can plant them directly into the soil.

A Romantic Crofter's Dream

My romantic crofter's dream is a lush and over-grown garden with trees and shrubs so close to the house that they almost hug the façade. Add a birdbath, a few pieces of run-down garden furniture, and an overgrown lawn, and you've created your new favorite "room."

Beautiful Terracotta Pots

I love good, old terracotta pots—so much so that I use them as the cachepot instead of as the inner pot. Before I plant in them, I soak the pots in a bucket overnight, so they absorb the water. If you want a beautiful patina on the pot, let it sit out the whole summer.

Additionally, if you brush or dab on a little yogurt, the terracotta becomes mottled white and very lovely.

Flowers for a Romantic Crofter's Style
- Bleeding Heart
- Musk Mallow
- Fire Lily
- Peonies
- Aquilegia
- Astrantia
- Poppies
- Hollyhock
- Monkshood

Grow in Pallet Collars

If you, like me, are a little lazy overall but you still want to grow in the garden, I recommend growing in pallet collars. We bought ours from a neighbor, but with a little luck, you can beg them from a lumberyard. Just make sure the wood is not impregnated.

Cover the bottom of the well with a ground cloth—this way, you can avoid all weeds. The earth in the pallet collars warms up faster, and the plantation height reaches a better working height. If you would like, you can cover the box with plastic or old window glass. Then it works like a small greenhouse.

Cutlery Flower Sticks

You can make flower sticks for the garden with old cutlery. Write with permanent marker on the blade of a knife or the handle of a fork. You can use a hammer to flatten a spoon and write on it.

Flower sticks make it easier in the beginning to distinguish vegetables, herbs, and flowers from the weeds.

Rose Sugar

Mix rose petals, lavender flowers, and lilac to make a super yummy sugar. Pick some flowers from the plant and put them on a white paper for an hour so that any small insects crawl out. Remove the flower's petals, and discard those that are damaged or brown. Then mix the flower petals with sugar in a tightly sealed jar. Leave it for a few weeks. Then remove the flowers by straining the sugar. Pour the sugar into a clean jar, and then use it in cookies, cakes, and other yummy things.

Clara's Nettle Soup

Nettles are a hated weed, but they have their uses, too. Of course, I love the burning leaves that feel really smooth if you pick them properly. As foods, the nettles are climate-friendly, nutritious, and free.

You Need:
70 oz (2 liters) delicate nettles
1 large yellow onion
2 cloves garlic
1–2 tsp salt
1 tbsp butter
1 ½ tbsp plain flour
50 oz (1 ½ liters) broth
salt and pepper
fresh herbs, such as basil or oregano
boiled eggs for serving (optional)

Instructions: Rinse the nettles and remove the stems. Blanch them quickly in boiling water. Remove the nettles and pour the water out.

Chop the nettles and onion, and fry them in butter in a large saucepan. Dust in the flour and add the broth. Boil for 5–10 minutes.

Season to taste, decorate the soup with basil leaves and a hefty dose of black pepper. With some egg halves, the soup becomes more filling. Serve with soft bread.

Other Edible Plants
• dandelion leaf
• sorrel
• violets

Apple Party in the Garden

I happily extend the feeling of summer by eating outdoors well into September. It works just fine if you have warm blankets on your lap. Outdoor furniture can be an expensive investment, but truthfully, ordinary furniture works just as well in the garden. Protect the tabletop by covering it with a tightly woven wax cloth that can be fastened under the tabletop.

Set the Table for a Party
An imaginary barrier to buying secondhand porcelain is that you might get mismatched sets. Personally, I prefer to set the table with uneven sets of porcelain, and if you stick to a uniform color scheme and style, it works perfectly. Here I have set the table with Finnish Arabia and Vinranka by Gustavsberg porcelain. Swirling and beautiful!

Set in small glasses, autumn's last flowers and spices make beautiful centerpieces. It's nice to have flowers on the table that don't block the view of your table companion or compete with the aromas of the food. I like the effect you get from using several mismatched vases together. In this case, I used a shot glass, cans, an old lantern, and—believe it or not—the bottom of an old glass breast pump!

Seating Labels
Autumnal fruit from the garden can be used for a lot of things. Here, I have used them as seating labels.

Instructions: Cut sheets of green card stock and write the names. Make a small hole with a needle and thread a string through the paper. Tie the string to the apple stem. Place the apples on the table.

WHAT YOU NEED:

- fall fruit
- thread
- green paper

Laces and the Like . . .

I get so sad when I see our cultural history sold off for nothing. Handmade lace, hand-woven linens, and small crocheted cloths that rarely cost more than a few dollars. I love to take care of these small works of art. The towels are unbeatable to dry the dishes with and are so beautiful that they might as well act as napkins in a rustic and festive table setting.

Strengthening lace with sugar or potato flour is traditional housewife methodology. Back in the olden days, it gave a bounce to petticoats, tablecloths, and shirt collars. At my house they're formed into bowls or, as here, napkin rings.

Instructions: Cut 5 inch (15 cm) long pieces of lace. Link the ends of the lace so that they form a circle. Mix powdered sugar with water, and stir until it is a viscous syrup. Soak the lace in the sugar solution, and squeeze out excess liquid. Drape the lace over small drinking glasses, and let dry overnight.

WHAT YOU NEED:

• lace
• ¾ cup (200 ml) powdered sugar
• ¼ cup (50 ml) water

TIP!
. . . .
You can also make beautiful bowls in the same way. I made the fruit dish in the picture from a round cloth soaked in the sugar solution, and then dried it on top of an upside-down bowl.

Apple Lanterns

Fruit lanterns are both beautiful and inexpensive. And they're particularly appropriate for an apple festival, of course! All you need is an apple and a tealight.

Instructions: Choose an apple that stands up stably, or cut off a piece from the bottom so that it doesn't wobble. Separate the candle from the aluminum mold, and punch out a circle in the apple by pressing the aluminum shape into the top of the apple. Cut with a knife along the mark, and carefully scoop out the circle with a teaspoon. Push down the tealight, and light it up. Beautiful!

Luscious Apple Pie

I got this fantastic recipe from my friend Sara. The pie has a sweet toffee flavor that works perfectly with tart apples.

You Need:

5 tart apples
10 tbsp (150 g) butter
¾ cup (200 ml) fiber-fortified oatmeal
¾ cup (200 ml) spelt flour
¾ cup (200 ml) muscovado sugar
¼ cup (50 ml) whipping cream
¼ cup (50 ml) syrup
½ tsp baking powder
2 tsp ground cardamom

Instructions: Preheat the oven to 350 degrees Fahrenheit (175 degrees Celcius). Melt the butter in a saucepan and stir in all the ingredients except the apples. Peel and cut the apples into wedges. Put the apple wedges in the bottom of a greased pie dish, and pour over the toffee mixture. Bake the pie in the center rack of the oven for about 25 minutes.

TIP!

Polishing silver does not need to be a hassle. Put the silver in a bowl lined with aluminum foil. Pour in boiling water and a generous amount of salt. In just a few seconds, the silver become spotless. It's unlikely there will be any hard-to-get stains left, but if there are, you can easily remove them with a little toothpaste. Dissolve stubborn stains about the house with baking soda and vinegar. Sprinkle baking soda on the stains, and then sprinkle that with vinegar. Let it bubble and fizz. When it stops, scrub it clean with a sponge.

Do More Composting

It's stupid to allow the nutrients from food scraps and household garbage to be hauled away and burned up. We have two large food composters in our garden where we dump household waste year-round. There's a lot of fussy advice about how to best manage a composter. This is great, but I prefer things to be simple. Sooner or later, the food breaks down anyway. If you doubt me, put food scraps in a barrel in the garden and try to prevent them from decomposing.

If you don't want to mix and water the compost regularly, you can do what I do and get a couple of composters so you can fill one at a time. When one is full, load the other one. Our composters are active and decompose throughout the long winter—except for a week in

February when the thermometer shows minus thirty-five. And every spring, we have a barrel full of fertile soil!

When I rake leaves in the fall, I usually don't compost them; rather I'll put them in the vegetable garden. By the spring, they'll have decomposed and made the soil beautiful and fluffy. All other garden debris—like sticks and branches—we usually burn in the fall.

My Best Gardening Activities
- Fertilizing the flower beds with composted earth
- Harvesting snow peas
- Lying in the hammock
- Picking strawberries

There Are No Right Answers

"Come and look guys!" I would shout to my family on Saturday evenings. They were dragged into my refurbished childhood room, where they got to walk around and admire. To rearrange and make things pretty has always been a passion of mine. Even back in the days when I only had one room seventy-five feet square to decorate, I tested all possible furniture arrangements to maximize results. But the result isn't even important. Rather, it's the ideas you have and how you implement them that count.

The room doesn't have to look better after you rearrange it. It's about being creative and making something different. I lie awake at night and ponder the curtains for the living room, and in the morning I rush up and start sewing. When the project's finished I get such an endorphin kick that lasts throughout the day. The kick comes from having taken a project through from conception to creation—not from whatever the end result looks like. And besides, you never get tired from having made something. I find you only get tired from what you have not done.

I strictly believe that you can never go wrong when you are being creative. The result may be ugly, impractical, clumsy, or distasteful. But never wrong. The fear of making mistakes keeps us from growing. This is linked to the idea that there is a right way, a correct answer. Nonsense! As if there were the right way to the Sistine Chapel.

My friend Anna told me of her experience in the first grade when she drew what her birthday was like. Anna drew flowers and packages, a large sun—the works—like you do when you're seven years old and love your birthday. When the teacher saw it, she told Anna, "In March there are no flowers. In March, there's snow and slush." Unbelievably hurt, Anna crumpled up her drawing and drew one with a red house. Outside the house was snow and slush. She then drew herself at a window with a large speech bubble that said "fucking teacher!" Today, Anna works as an artist and illustrator. How fortunate that at the age of seven she already knew to create independently and think outside the box. There is no correct path to creativity. We have to create our own paths and invent our own solutions.

Index

Thanks

to all my blog readers—you who just found your way there when I started blogging a hundred years ago. It's thanks to you that my book has become a reality! And the fact that you're reading, cheering, and commenting—it's all worth gold to me. And thanks to my grandmother, who taught me to appreciate the great in the small and to take advantage of what I have instead of throwing things away and buying something new. You were before your time, and society ran away from you. You're now the height of fashion!

www.skyhorsepublishing.com
10 9 8 7 6 5 4 3 2 1

Library of Congress Cataloging-in-Publication Data is available on file.

ISBN: 978-1-62636-103-4
Printed in China